Eyes WIDE *Open*
Healing Group

PARTICIPANT GUIDE

Living in Truth Ministries

Eyes Wide Open Healing Group Participant Guide

This healing group program coincides with Kimberly Davidson's book *Eyes Wide Open: Love Yourself & Love Your Body in 9-weeks (Special Edition)*

Please Note: This healing group program is not a replacement for professional treatment.

Learn more information at: LivingInTruthMinistries.com

Table of Contents

Introduction Letter

Welcome to Eyes Wide Open!

Did you know that only 4% of women around the world consider themselves beautiful? The truth is every woman is a beautiful and unique reflection of her Creator and God has a plan and purpose for her life. Like flowers, women come in different shapes, colors, and sizes, adding unique fragrance to the world. This *Eyes Wide Open* healing group program will help you see yourself through God's eyes, embrace your unique beauty, and find true and lasting freedom from your struggles with food & body-image.

Disordered eating is a serious problem in our culture today and affects millions of women in the U.S. alone. Many secular-based programs address the physical and psychological components of disordered eating but they neglect an equally important component—spiritual.

The Bible tells us that we have been created in God's image. But what does that really mean? In the same way that Father, Son, and Spirit make up the whole of who God is our mind, body, and spirit make up the whole of who God created us to be. Neglecting to address any part of who God created us to be leads to incomplete healing.

Struggles with food and body-image can sometimes turn into what the Bible calls a stronghold, something which you feel powerless to overcome on your own. The key to recovery from strongholds lies in the renewed mind (Romans 12:1-2). We accomplish a renewed mind when we replace worldly lies with the timeless truths found in Scripture.

Those involved in these healing groups are learning and growing with a common goal in mind—freedom in Christ. *"Then you will know the truth, and the truth will set you free" ~John 8:32!* This 10-week journey is one you will never forget. Are you ready to get started? Roll up your sleeves, remove your mask, and step boldly into the unknown. God will meet you where you are and lead you step by step.

Before you begin this journey visit **LivingInTruthMinistries.com/subscribe.** You will receive encouragment once a week as well as a **FREE eBook:** *Who Am I Really? A 12-Day Journey to Discover Your True Identity.*

Note from Kimberly

Hello Ladies,

I'm so excited to hear you will be journeying through *Eyes Wide Open*. It takes courage to come forward and be willing to be transparent and vulnerable.

There is a living God and He cares and loves you. It is my intention and hope that you have a personal encounter with your Creator, the One who heals the wounded. God is genuinely interested in you. You can release your past and pursue your future through a personal healing journey with Him.

Both secular and faith-based medical and mental health professionals agree that if faith and hope are high, the recovery process will most likely be successful. One of the misconceptions is, "I'll have to struggle for the rest of my life." I am one of many women who over time returned to normal eating parameters. You can too. In the beginning you may feel that nothing is happening. Or you say, "I don't want to go there!" You will discover that something amazing is happening. Go there! Hang in there. It is worth it. God's Word says that God will work out His plans for your life (Psalm 138:8).

There is no area in your life so painful, no offense so heinous, that God's grace cannot heal it. The mistakes of your past need not determine your future. God can bring beauty out of your darkest secrets. I am living proof that God can miraculously transform what society labels as broken and dysfunctional into someone new and functional. God restored what sin stole. His promise, "I will repay you for the years the locusts have eaten … You will have plenty to eat, until you are full, and you will praise the name of the LORD your God, who has worked wonders for you; never again will my people be shamed" (Joel 2:25-26) became a reality.

I will be praying for you! "The Lord is the Spirit who gives them life, and where he is there is freedom" (2 Corinthians 3:17, TLB).

Blessings in Him,

Kimberly Davidson, MA, BCBC
Pastoral Counselor, Spiritual Development Coach, Author, Speaker
Facebook Fan page: Kimberly Davidson, Author
Web: www.OliveBranchOutreach.com

My Recovery Story

By Rae Lynn DeAngelis

God has a plan for each of our lives. Unfortunately, Satan also has a plan for us, a plan that includes keeping us held prisoner by his lies and deception.

The world would have us believe we have no control over such things, that we are just helpless victims. I have come to believe, however, this is yet another one of Satan's lies—a lie that keeps us in bondage even longer.

I'm so thankful God has shown me the truth. Although we may become prisoners, the prison door is often locked from the inside. God is waiting for us to come to Him, so that He can show us where the key is hidden and set us free.

> Likewise the tongue is a small part of the body, but it makes great boasts. Consider what a great forest is set on fire by a small spark. The tongue is also a fire, a world of evil among the parts of the body. It corrupts the whole person, sets the whole course of his life on fire, and is itself set on fire by hell (James 3:5-6).

Is this Scripture ever true! Words were the very thing Satan used to draw me into his world of lies and deception.

At a very young age, the enemy began planting lies in my mind—lies that eventually produced a twenty-five year bondage to an eating disorder called bulimia. It saddens me to think that Satan would prey upon such innocence, but he ruthless and evil. (The mind of a child is vulnerable and the enemy of our soul knows it.) Growing up he took advantage of certain circumstances in my life and began to bend my mind into believing that I could only be loved if I was thin.

One of my earliest childhood memories is from the age of three. Even at this young age, I can remember having negative feelings about my body image. I had two best friends in the neighborhood where I grew up and they were both tiny and petite. I was average size. I started comparing myself to them, and because I was bigger than them, I determined that I must be fat.

As I got a bit older, I really did start to become chubby. Kids can be cruel. Their hurtful words and comments took a toll on my self-esteem. My self-worth dwindled even more when people in my own family commented on my weight. My grandma would often remark on how fat I was getting. I don't believe she intentionally meant to hurt me. Maybe she thought I needed motivation to lose weight. Regardless of her reasons the result was that I felt awful about myself.

I remember one time my dad had bargained with me that if I lost weight, he would buy me a whole new wardrobe. I now realize he was only trying to help, but at the time I believed I wasn't acceptable to him as I was. I thought he would love me better if I was thin. Please know that I do not blame my dad in any way. He was simply a product of his own upbringing. He came from a family that never had to deal with weight issues and so he had no real understanding of how I felt.

The enemy took full advantage of the situation, however, and as a result, I believed his lie. *I could not be loved as I was. I needed to be thin.*

Age ten was a traumatic time in my life. It was at this age that I started my menstrual cycle, which made me even more self-conscious about my body. The physical changes I was experiencing caused me to feel even more isolated. Most of the kids at that age were not anywhere near puberty yet.

Not only did I feel fat, but I grew extremely self-conscious about my body. These factors alone were enough to cause my self-esteem to plummet. But there was more. At this same tender age of ten the most traumatic thing in my life occurred. *A relative molested me.*

This was someone who was supposed to protect me, someone I loved and trusted.

If there was one day that I could completely clear from my past, this day would be it. That tragic event ripped something away from my inner-soul that I can never get back. Childhood sexual abuse, to any extent, is devastating and life altering. I was forever changed, and once again Satan was right there with his lies. He convinced me that it was somehow my fault. I was an emotional mess. The sad part is I didn't get to be a child for very long.

After the incident, this relative begged me to not tell anyone, but after much urging from my mom when she sensed something was very wrong, I spilled the ugly truth. Believing they were protecting me from further harm, my parents honored my plea for secrecy and made sure I was never left alone with this adult again.

I really felt awful about my body after this and tried to gain control by losing weight. I didn't do it the right way. I severly restricted my food intake, which caused me to lose some weight, but as soon as I started eating again, I would gain the weight back.

Then one day, I overheard my parents talking about a friend's niece who had an eating disorder. (It was the first time I had heard about such a thing.) My parents said the girl would barely eat, and that when she did eat, she would make herself throw up.

This is how warped my thinking was at that time. I actually thought to myself: *Wow, you can do that; you can eat and then get rid of it?*

This marked the beginning of my eating disorder. Bulimia followed me all the way through my teens, all the way through my twenties, and most of the way through my thirties. I can't tell you how many times I tried to stop, but my resolve never lasted long. I convinced myself that I had it all under control, but it literally controlled me. No one knew the lie I was living, and I did everything I could to keep it a secret. Deep down I knew that what I was doing was wrong, but my fear of gaining weight was too great.

The enemy planted so many lies in my head. I believed I would not be loved if I gained weight. I also believed that I would never be able to eat like a normal person.

So, I eventually decided that this was just something I was going to have to live with for the rest of my life.

Thankfully, that's not the end of my story.

By my mid-thirties, I thought my life was on the right track. God had brought me to a place where I had grown a lot as a Christian woman. I was very involved at my church, both in service and in studying His Word. Eventually, I got to a place where I wanted more from my relationship with God. I wanted to go deeper, but for some reason I just couldn't get there.

Then God revealed to me why. I still had this huge secret I was carrying around with my eating disorder and God made it very clear. If I wanted to get to the next level with Him, I needed to confront this out of control monster and make some changes in my life.

It seems like the closer I grow in my relationship with God, the more sin I discover in my life. I guess God reveals our sin when He knows we are strong enough to handle it. Little by little He reveals our sin so we can weed it from our lives.

The thought of trying to weed this sin out terrified me. It had been a part of my everyday life for so long; I honestly couldn't comprehend how to do it.

"Since we have these promises, dear friends, let us purify ourselves from everything that contaminates body and spirit, perfecting holiness out of reverence for God" (2 Corinthians 7:1).

I couldn't see how I would ever be free from bulimia and had no idea where to begin, but God's Word reassured me. "Do not be afraid. Stand firm, and you will see the deliverance the LORD will bring you today" (Exodus 14:13).

God had already laid the groundwork for my healing. I had been part of a Bible study with the same women for about two years and realized that if I was going to get better, I needed to tell someone about my problem. It needed to be someone I could trust and someone who would hold me accountable for my actions. I finally confided in one of my closest friends. She then encouraged me to talk with the six women in my bible study group. Eventually, I mustered up the courage to seek their help as well.

God placed these seven women in my life (God's perfect number I might add) to help me get better. They became pillars of strength and encouragement; they were God's audible voice and His loving arms that I so desperately needed.

"So do not fear, for I am with you; do not be dismayed, for I am your God. I will strengthen you and help you; I will uphold you with my righteous right hand" (Isaiah 41:10).

By no coincidence, my study group decided to work through a Bible study by Beth Moore called *Breaking Free*. The premise of the study is learning to break free from strongholds in your life through the renewed mind.

Romans 12:2 says "Do not conform any longer to the pattern of this world, but be transformed by the renewing of your mind."

Renewing the mind takes time and effort. It is a process that involves identifying the many lies we have believed about ourselves and replacing those lies with truth—God's truth.

My personal mind renewal process included writing out relevant Scriptures on index cards and reading through them every day.

I was making some progress but still clung to my eating disorder behavior at times. I couldn't completely break free, and I couldn't understand why.

After two and a half decades, I finally found the key that would unlock my prison door. It was found through a story in the Gospel of Mark where a man brings his demon-possessed son to Jesus to be healed.

Jesus asked the boy's father, "How long has he been like this?" "From childhood, he answered. "It has often thrown him into the fire or water to kill him. But if you can do anything, take pity on us and help us." "If you can?" Jesus said. "Everything is possible for him who believes." Immediately the boy's father exclaimed, "I do believe; help me overcome my unbelief" (Mark 9:21-24)!

At that moment it hit me! I realized that my biggest problem was unbelief. I wasn't fully convinced that God really could heal me. So I began praying every day, *"God help me overcome my unbelief."*

Little by little, I began trusting God with my eating disorder. And after many months of prayer, mind renewal, and taking baby steps towards recovery, I was finally ready to let go.

I said, "All right God, I am going to take you at your Word and believe you can heal me." (Guess what? God was always capable; He was just waiting for me to believe it.) Since that day bulimia has no longer been my burden to carry. I have completely given it over to God, the only one capable of taking it from me.

"Therefore, if anyone is in Christ, he is a new creation; the old has gone, the new has come! All of this is from God, who reconciled us to himself through Christ and gave us the ministry of reconciliation" (2 Corinthians 5:17-18).

I decided that I needed a visual reminder I was a changed person, so I colored my hair brown. That may seem silly to you, but it really did help. Every time I looked in the mirror, I was reminded of the healing God gave me. After a few years, I no longer needed that outward reminder of my inward change and went back to being a blonde.

Looking back, I realize how crucial God's Word was to my recovery. I began to really think through the importance of replacing Satan's lies with God's truth.

Replacing lies with truth became a battle in my mind—a battle with the enemy himself. Ephesians chapter six explains that when we go into battle with Satan, we need to put on the full armor of God.

Therefore put on the full armor of God, so that when the day of evil comes, you may be able to stand your ground, and after you have done everything, to stand. Stand firm then, with the belt of truth buckled around you waist, with the breastplate of righteousness in place, and with your feet fitted with the readiness that comes from the gospel of peace. In addition to all this, take up the shield of faith, with which you can extinguish all the flaming arrows of the evil one. Take up the helmet of salvation and the sword of the Spirit, which is the word of God (Ephesians 6:13-17).

All the parts of armor described in this passage are for our defense and protection. However, the Sword of the Spirit is unique. It provides more than protection. It is the means through which we can offensively attack the lies of Satan.

"For the word of God is living and active. Sharper than any double-edged sword, it penetrates even to dividing soul and spirit, joints and marrow; it judges the thoughts and attitudes of the heart" (Hebrews 4:12).

God enables us to wield the Sword with authority and power!

Our weapon of choice is the Sword of the Spirit. But how can we know for sure that Satan really is lying to us?

I have found that the enemy always leaves visible fingerprints when he lies. Those fingerprints include *secrecy, shame, distortion, deception,* and *fear.* As I reflect back on my own experience, I can now see those fingerprints clearly. But thankfully, I have learned that for every lie Satan dishes out, God counters it with the truth of His Word.

I would like to share with you a few lies the enemy used to deceive me—along with the truths God has equipped me.

SECRECY - Satan's lie: *If anyone knew the truth about me, they would be disgusted; they wouldn't want anything to do with me.*
- **God's Truth:** "When I am afraid, I will trust in you. In God, whose word I praise, in God I trust; I will not be afraid. What can mortal man do to me"(Psalm 56:3-4)?

SHAME – Satan's lie: *How can I face people once they know the real me?*
- **God's Truth:** "As Scripture says, "Anyone who trusts in him will never be put to shame" (Romans 10:11).

DECEPTION - Satan's lie: *Who am I kidding? Why would God want to waste his time on me of all people?*
- **God's Truth**: "Because [she] loves me," says the LORD, "I will rescue [her]; I will protect [her], for [she] acknowledges my name. [She] will call upon me, and I will answer [her]; I will be with [her] in trouble, I will deliver [her] and honor [her]" (Psalm 91:14-15). [Gender emphasis mine]

DISTORTION – Satan's lie: *With a past like mine, I'll never be of any use to God.*
- **God's Truth:** "Here is a trustworthy saying that deserves full acceptance: Christ Jesus came into the world to save sinners-of whom I am the worst. But for that reason I was shown mercy so that in me, the worst of sinners, Christ

Jesus might display his unlimited patience as an example for those who would believe on him and receive eternal life" (1 Timothy 1:15-16).

FEAR – Satan's lie: *I'll never be completely free from this; it's going to haunt me for the rest of my life.*

- **God's Truth:** "For this reason I remind you to fan into flame the gift of God, which is in you through the laying on of my hands. For God did not give us a spirit of timidity, but a spirit of power, of love and of self-discipline" (2 Timothy 1:6-7).

"So do not throw away your confidence; you will be richly rewarded. You need to persevere so that when you have done the will of God, you will receive what he has promised" (Hebrews 10:35-36).

I am completely awed by God's grace; He was so patient. He never gave up on me, even though I had given up on myself. It comforts me to know that throughout everything I had experienced God was right there with me. He knew exactly what went wrong and how I had become so broken. Jesus met me right where I was and had compassion on me. He was with me when the hurtful things were said. He was with me when the person I trusted stole my innocence. And He was there to set me free!

God continues to replace the enemy's lies with His unchanging truths. Thanks to Almighty God - I am free! The Lord saved me, and I am forever grateful.

"It is for freedom that Christ has set us free. Stand firm, then, and do not let yourselves be burdened again by a yoke of slavery" (Galatians 5:1).

ABOUT THE AUTHOR

After God set Rae Lynn free, He called her to go and help others find freedom. She is both the Founder and Executive Direcor of Living in Truth Ministries and is passionate about helping woman embrace their unique identity and see themselves through God's eyes. Her goal is to help women replace lies with truth and live in freeom. Rae Lynn's captivating message of hope and healing through the Great Physicain, Jesus Christ, encourages and inspires women around the world.

If you have not done so already, be sure to visit **LivingInTruthMinistries.com** for some great resources to support your healing journey:

CONFIDENTIALITY & LIMITATION OF SERVICES AGREEMENT

1. I understand the services provided through this group are not a substitute for medical, psychological, or dietetic care and that the volunteer facilitators offer Christian support through the counsel of God's Word and personal experience.

2. I understand that this program is recommended to be used as a supplement (not replacement) to professional care. It is my responsibility to obtain additional support through the professional resources available in my community.

3. I am aware that while a wide range of education and experience is represented through the leaders of this support group, they are only volunteers - not professionals.

4. If at any time I become overwhelmed, and feel my physical or mental health is at serious risk, I will seek additional help through physical or mental health professionals available in my community.

5. I understand this program does not come with a guarantee; healing takes time and varies from person to person.

6. I will do my best to attend weekly meetings and complete homework assignments.

7. I will respect the privacy of group members and leaders and agree to keep anything spoken during group time confidential.

I_____ have read the Limitation of Service/Confidentiality Agreement; I understand and agree to the guidelines set forth there-in.

_____
(Signature)

_____
(Date)

NOTE: Fill out this form and return it to your leader. (hardcopy, scan, photo)

Story Week
Introduction

Open with prayer

Participant: Introduce yourself, and give one word to describe how you are feeling during this present season of your life.

Ground Rules: (Review these ground rules before each meeting)
1) I'll be a great listener.
2) I'll be honest.
3) What happens in the group stays in the group.
4) I'll share stories instead of advice.
5) I'll be prepared for each group.
6) We will end this group on time!

➤ **MEETING FORMAT** refer to Week One outline
   o **Scriptures for Renewing the Mind:** copy into index card booklets each week, read daily, & be prepared to share with group which one spoke to you most
   o **2 Steps Forward—1 Step Back:** share successes and challenges from the past week in relation to your healing journey
   o **Discussion:** is built off of reading material and questions in EWO guide
   o **Action Challenge:** At the end of week's outline answer the questions: What is God saying to me? What am I going to do about it?

<u>**Share Your Story:**</u> Sharing time should be kept to **five minutes or less** (use the timer on your smartphone or iPad if necessary)
   o **What to share:** Share a little bit about your past in relation to your reason for participating in this group, where you are today, and what you hope to gain from this program?

Homework (Read all of Week-1 in Kimberly's book and answer the daily questions on the Week-1 outline. Write Week-1 Scriptures for Renewing the Mind into your index card booklet.)

Close with prayer

Discover the Character of God
Week #1

Scriptures for Renewing the Mind: Copy into index card booklets and read through every day.

- "I am God, and there is no other; I am God, and there is none like me" **(Isaiah 46:9).**

- "Trust in the LORD with all your heart and lean not on your own understanding; in all your ways submit to him, and he will make your paths straight" **(Proverbs 3:5-6).**

Discussion Questions

At the beginning of week one, Kimberly highlights five different women with five different struggles. With whom do you most relate and why?

Day One: What is your current view of God and how would you like to see Him differently?

Day Two: What are some ways you've struggled in relationship with your earthly father?

Day Three: What feels especially heavy to your right now? What do you do to deaden the pain?

Day Four: "Knowing" God has less to do with head knowledge (which comes from books) and has more to do with heart knowledge (which comes from life-experience). What life-experiences have shaped your current perspective of God?

Day Five: In what ways do you currently feel uncertain or unworthy of God's love?

Good Father Exercise: Take a few minutes to brainstorm as a group, naming as many character traits as you can think of which would best describe a good earthly father? (Make sure everyone has a chance to participate.) As a leader, jot these down in the space below. Afterwards, read them aloud, one-by-one, and ask the group which of these traits can be applied to character of God.

Action Challenge: What is God saying to me, and what am I going to do about it?

NOTE: You will be paired with an **Encouragement Buddy** each week. Below are some suggestions for how you can interact with one another:
- Pray for one another
- Send an encouraging text, email, song or video, phone call
- Discuss homework
- Hold one another accountable for completing homework assignments, attending weekly meetings, and taking steps forward with their action challenge

Pursue Perfection God's Way
Week #2

Scriptures for Renewing the Mind: Copy into index card booklets and read through every day.

- "Listen, O daughter, consider and give ear: Forget your people and your father's house. The king is enthralled by your beauty; honor him, for he is your Lord" **(Psalm 45:10-12).**

- "The LORD does not look at the things people look at. People look at the outward appearance, but the LORD looks at the heart" **(1 Samuel 16:7b).**

Discussion Questions

Day One: What outside influences have shaped your perception of how you think you should look?

Day Two: Which areas of your life do you find yourself striving for perfection?

Day Three: How has your unhealthy thoughts or behaviors around food or body-image damaged your relationships with God and others?

Day Four: Kimberly has an interesting acronym for DENIAL: Don't Even Notice I Am Lying. What are some lies you have told yourself or others in order to conceal your struggles with food or body-image?

Day Five: What people or circumstances cause feelings of jealousy or envy to rise up within you?

Mask Exercise: On pages 25-26 you will find two masks. On the "outside" of the mask write words that describe how you want others to perceive you. On the "inside" of the mask write words that describe how you perceive yourself. Share with the group what you wrote. It is a powerful demonstration that reveals we all have insecure feelings about ourselves yet many people go through life wearing masks to disguise their true feelings.

Action Challenge: What is God saying to me, and what am I going to do about it?

NOTE: You will be paired with an **Encouragement Buddy** each week. Below are some suggestions for how you can interact with one another:
- o Pray for one another
- o Send an encouraging text, email, song or video, phone call
- o Discuss homework
- o Hold one another accountable for completing homework assignments, attending weekly meetings, and taking steps forward with their action challenge

Why Do I Hurt?
Week #3

Scriptures for Renewing the Mind: (copy into index card booklets and read every day)

- "Because [she] loves me," says the LORD, "I will rescue [her]; I will protect [her], for [she] acknowledges my name. [She] will call upon me, and I will answer [her]; I will be with [her] in trouble, I will deliver [her] and honor [her]" **(Psalm 91:14-15).** [Gender emphasis added]

- "So do not fear, for I am with you; do not be dismayed, for I am your God. I will strengthen you and help you; I will uphold you with my righteous right hand" **(Isaiah 41:10).**

- "And we know that in all things God works for the good of those who love him, who have been called according to his purpose" **(Romans 8:28).**

- "And the God of all grace, who called you to his eternal glory in Christ, after you have suffered a little while, will himself make you strong, firm and steadfast" **(1 Peter 5:10).**

Discussion Questions

At the beginning of week two, Kimberly talked about her scare with optical neuritis. Have you had any close calls or serious complications resulting from your disordered eating? Please explain.

Day One: What regrets do you have from the past, and what fears do you have of tomorrow?

Day Two: Read Mark 5:25-43. In what ways can you relate to the bleeding woman?

Day Three: Have you ever gone through the refining process (described in Kimberly's book) with God? Please explain.

Day Four: What are some of the things that God has pruned (cut away) from your life? How has this impacted you emotionally, spiritually, and/or relationally?

Day Five: Based on your current knowledge of the life of Jesus, what are some ways He might be able relate to your personal struggles?

Action Challenge: What is God saying to me, and what am I going to do about it?

NOTE: You will be paired with an **Encouragement Buddy** each week. Below are some suggestions for how you can interact with one another:
- o Pray for one another
- o Send an encouraging text, email, song or video, phone call
- o Discuss homework
- o Hold one another accountable for completing homework assignments, attending weekly meetings, and taking steps forward with their action challenge

The Beauty of Truth

Week #4

Scriptures for Renewing the Mind: (copy into index card booklets and read every day)

- "We demolish arguments and every pretension that sets itself up against the knowledge of God, and we take captive every thought to make it obedient to Christ" (**2 Corinthians 10:5).**

- "For the word of God is living and active. Sharper than any double-edged sword, it penetrates even to dividing soul and spirit, joints and marrow; it judges the thoughts and attitudes of the heart" **(Hebrews 4:12).**

- "Therefore put on the full armor of God, so that when the day of evil comes, you may be able to stand your ground, and after you have done everything, to stand" **(Ephesians 6:13).**

Discussion Questions

Day One: What are some of your greatest fears?

Day Two: Kimberly talked about depression and isolation as well as feelings of guilt and shame. In what ways can you relate to these things?

Day Three: Satan is the father of all lies. From the excerpt of C.S. Lewis' *The Screwtapes Letters,* can you identify any similar lies of the enemy (Satan) in your own life? Explain.

Day Four: From the list of lies provided, which ones have you bought into? After you have identified the lies, look up the truths that counter those lies and add them to your index card booklet.

Day Five: Read Luke 4:1-12. What insight can you take from this passage and apply towards your own life?

Action Challenge: What is God saying to me, and what am I going to do about it?

NOTE: You will be paired with an **Encouragement Buddy** each week. Below are some suggestions for how you can interact with one another:
- o Pray for one another
- o Send an encouraging text, email, song or video, phone call
- o Discuss homework
- o Hold one another accountable for completing homework assignments, attending weekly meetings, and taking steps forward with their action challenge

Anger Is a Choice

Week #5

Scriptures for Renewing the Mind: (copy into index card booklets and read every day)

- "My dear brothers, take note of this; everyone should be quick to listen, slow to speak and slow to become angry, for man's anger does not bring about the righteous life that God desires" **(James 1:19-20).**

- ""But you, O LORD, are a God merciful and gracious, slow to anger and abounding in steadfast love and faithfulness" **(Psalm 86:15).**

- "Search me, O God, and know my heart; test me and know my anxious thoughts. See if there is any offensive way in me, and lead me in the way everlasting" **(Psalms 139:23-24).**

PLEASE NOTE: This week has six days of homework so be sure to plan accordingly.

Discussion Questions

Day One: What did you learn about God's anger from this day's reading?

Day Two: Based on the examples of Jesus in the Bible, what steps do you need to take in order to better control your anger.

Day Three: Using the examples given in Kimberly's book, which kinds of situations evoke the most anger in you?

Day Four: How did your parents or caregivers express anger growing up, how do you personally express anger, and how would you like to express anger differently?

Day Five: If you are harboring angry feelings towards God, confess them to Him, and then ask Him for wisdom and insight concerning the things you don't understand.

Day Six: Grieve the Losses. Make a list of your greatest losses and anyone you are holding responsible for it. Write a letter to God and ask Him to help you work through the grieving process over the next days, weeks, or months.

Action Challenge: What is God saying to me, and what am I going to do about it?

NOTE: You will be paired with an **Encouragement Buddy** each week. Below are some suggestions for how you can interact with one another:
- o Pray for one another
- o Send an encouraging text, email, song or video, phone call
- o Discuss homework
- o Hold one another accountable for completing homework assignments, attending weekly meetings, and taking steps forward with their action challenge

Freedom through Forgiveness
Week # 6

Scriptures for Renewing the Mind: (copy into index card booklets and read every day)

- "Therefore, as God's chosen people, holy and dearly loved, clothe yourselves with compassion, kindness, humility, gentleness, and patience. Bear with each other and forgive whatever grievances you may have against one another. Forgive as the Lord forgave you" **(Colossians 3: 12-13).**

- "Then Jesus said to his disciples, "If anyone would come after me, he must deny himself and take up his cross and follow me. For whoever wants to save his life will lose it, but whoever loses his life for me will find it" **(Matthew 16:24-25).**

PLEASE NOTE: This week has six days of homework so be sure to plan accordingly

Discussion Questions

Day One: What is your greatest battle with forgiveness today?

Day Two: Complete this sentence: I want to forgive [person] but what's holding me back is....

Day Three: Based on today's reading what misconceptions have you had about forgiveness?

Day Four: How does the story of Joseph forgiving his brothers encourage you today?

Day Five: Using the guidelines and sample letter following this week's outline, write a forgiveness letter in the space provided to someone you need to forgive. Be prepared to share your letter with the group

Day Six: From the seven practical steps for restoring and rebuilding a relationship, which steps do you feel most called to take at this time?

Action Challenge: What is God saying to me, and what am I going to do about it?

NOTE: You will be paired with an **Encouragement Buddy** each week. Below are some suggestions for how you can interact with one another:
- Pray for one another
- Send an encouraging text, email, song or video, phone call
- Discuss homework
- Hold one another accountable for completing homework assignments, attending weekly meetings, and taking steps forward with their action challenge

How to Write a Forgiveness Letter

Suggested Steps:

- Affirm any positives in the relationship. (Thank you for...)
- List specific grievances and express your choice to forgive. (I forgive you for...)
- Recognize and rebuke the enemy's control and lies. (Satan, you no longer have power over...)
- Pray for God's protection. (God, I ask you to protect...)
- Acknowledge and seek forgiveness for your own grievances. (Please forgive me for...)
- Pray for God's future blessings and peace. (God, I ask your blessings and peace over...)

Sample Letter:

Mom and Dad,

Thank you for being incredible parents who loved us, who gave us children a great heritage, work ethic, and you exemplified how important family is. I know that you did the best that you could at the time. All of your children love the Lord and that is a testament to your faithfulness and your obedience to Christ. Thank you for introducing me to the Holy Spirit and for bringing me up in a community of awesome pastors and friends.

I forgive you for teaching me how to love food and turn to food for comfort, for not educating me in health and balance when it comes to food. I forgive you for banning sugar from our house because it caused me to have an addiction to it. I forgive you for looking to food for comfort and celebration rather than praising God and looking to Him to fulfill my desires. I forgive you for teaching me how to cope and feel deprived so that I would have to cling to brownies and sugar like it was my god.

Satan, I tell you that you no longer have power over my family. The spirit of addiction to sugar, the spirit of emotional eating, the spirit of depression, the spirit of low self-esteem must leave our family in the name of Jesus. I command the spirit of rejection and unloving and bitterness to be gone. I pray that any agreements that we have made with these demons would be banished in the name of Jesus. Spirits you have to scat and get out of here. Your assignment has been cancelled and it stops right here and right now. You must go in the name of Jesus; you are UNWELCOME. You have no control and no power over me, my mouth, my thoughts, my stomach, my head, or my life in the name of Jesus, and I tell the spirit to stay away from my family; they belong to Jesus. I pray protection over their mind and heart.

God, I ask you to send your angels to camp around my family and they would take a stand against the evil one. I tell the spirit of binging, OCD, pride and judgement to be gone from this and future generations, in the name of Jesus. I break all roots with these spirits and command them to be cut off right now.

Holy Spirit, I'm inviting you into all of these areas. Bring healing and a sound mind to each member of my family. Bring your sense of peace and self-awareness to us. Be present and enable us to change. Help us be brave and stand up against the enemy. I pray that you teach us to come to you for comfort and strength and hope. I pray that we come to you with offering our bodies as living sacrifices. Please forgive us for gluttony. Please forgive us for not loving ourselves the way you do.

I speak blessings over this and future generations. I pray a blessing that our relationship with food can be healthy and balanced. I pray that we can look to you for true health and healing in the deepest wounds that we carry, that we would bring all emotions to you. I pray a blessing that joy and community and true communion with the Holy Spirit would be our healing and that your peace would cover over my entire family.

I ask these things through the authority of Jesus, the Son of God. Amen

Forgiveness Letter

Choosing Self-Discovery Over Control

Week #7

Scriptures for Renewing the Mind: (copy into index card booklets and read every day)

- "This is what the LORD says to you: "Do not be afraid or discouraged because of this vast army. For the battle is not yours, but God's" **(2 Chronicles 20:15).**

- "You will not have to fight this battle. Take up your positions; stand firm and you will see the deliverance the Lord will give you O Judah and Jerusalem. Do not be afraid; do not be discouraged. Go out to face them tomorrow, and the Lord will be with you"
(2 Chronicles 20:17).

- "If we confess our sins, he is faithful and just and will forgive us our sins and purify us from all unrighteousness" **(1 John 1:9).**

- "When I am afraid, I will trust in you. In God, whose word I praise, in God I trust; I will not be afraid. What can mortal man do to me" **(Psalm 56:3-4)?**

Discussion Questions

Day One: What kinds of experiences, people, or situations make you feel out of control, fearful, or threatened?

Day Two: Jesus focused on the end result rather than the painful process. What would you like your life to look like on the other side of recovery? Be as specific as you can.

Day Three: When you look back over your life, can you see how certain parts of your story were necessary in order to bring you to where you are today?

Day Four: From the list of deadly sins that include descriptions in Kimberly's book, which do you tend to struggle with the most?

Day Five: Satan has power when things are kept a secret, but the moment we confess our sins and get them out into the open, not only do we feel liberated, but the enemy loses so much power over our lives. Would you be willing to share with your group one secret that you've been keeping in the darkness? Take some time to pray about it this week, and if you feel it's time, bring your secret into the light by sharing it with your group.

Action Challenge: What is God saying to me, and what am I going to do about it?

NOTE: You will be paired with an **Encouragement Buddy** each week. Below are some suggestions for how you can interact with one another:
- o Pray for one another
- o Send an encouraging text, email, song or video, phone call
- o Discuss homework
- o Hold one another accountable for completing homework assignments, attending weekly meetings, and taking steps forward with their action challenge

Scriptures for Renewing the Mind: (copy into index card booklets and read every day)

- "Do not conform any longer to the pattern of this world, but be transformed by the renewing of your mind" **(Romans 12:2).**

- "Watch and pray so that you will not fall into temptation" **(Matthew 26:41).**

- "Do you not know that your body is a temple of the Holy Spirit, who is in you, whom you have received from God? You are not your own; you were bought at a price. Therefore honor God with your body" **(1 Corinthians 6:19-20).**

Discussion Questions

Day One: What social pressures have you found yourself conforming to?

Day Two: What triggers tempt you to act on your unhealthy behaviors or negative body image feelings?
- Share what emotions/feelings are usually associated with your times of temptation?

- Share times or places you are most tempted.

Day Three: Have you ever met someone who didn't meet the stereotypical standards of beauty yet they radiated a kind of beauty all their own? What was it about that person that made them so attractive to you? What does that tell you about where true beauty comes from?

Day Four: Read **Romans 6:19-23**. How is this passage speaking to your heart today?

Day Five: What do your current relationships look like? Take inventory:

o   Which relationships do you need to let go of because they are unhealthy?

o   Which relationships do you need to build into because they are healthy?

Action Challenge: What is God saying to me, and what am I going to do about it?

NOTE: You will be paired with an **Encouragement Buddy** each week. Below are some suggestions for how you can interact with one another:
- o   Pray for one another
- o   Send an encouraging text, email, song or video, phone call
- o   Discuss homework
- o   Hold one another accountable for completing homework assignments, attending weekly meetings, and taking steps forward with their action challenge

Scriptures for Renewing the Mind: (copy into index card booklets and read every day)

- "Forget the former things; do not dwell on the past. See, I am doing a new thing! Now it springs up; do you not perceive it? I am making a way in the desert and streams in the wasteland" **(Isaiah 43:18-19).**

- "Then I heard the voice of the Lord saying, "Whom shall I send? And who will go for us?" And I said, "Here am I, send me" **(Isaiah 6:8)!**

- "Your word is a lamp to my feet and a light for my path" **(Psalm 119:105).**

- "Arise, shine, for your light has come, and the glory of the Lord rises upon you" **(Isaiah 60:1).**

Discussion Questions

Day One: Read Acts 9:1-22. What parallels or hope can you draw from Paul's conversion and apply to your own life?

New Name Exercise: Just as Saul received a new name/identity after his encounter with Jesus on the road to Damascus, during your next meeting, you will receive a new name/identity to celebrate the conclusion of your journey through this program. (All of the new names with accompanying scriptures can be found at the end of this week's outline.)

Day Two: Which Scriptures about your identity on this day do you need to cling to most right now?

Day Three: Part of your continuing healing journey includes reaching out to help others who are struggling. Would you consider helping others in their healing journey by facilitating a future *Eyes Wide Open* group?

Day Four: What has been the most impactful in your healing journey as you have come through this program? Share any ah ha moments. Share what God is doing in your heart and spirit since coming through this program.

Day Five: Read the Ralph Martson quote from this day in Kimberly's book. What encouragement can you take away this and apply to your own life?

Action Challenge: What is God saying to me, and what am I going to do about it?

PLEASE NOTE: As this group closes, be sure to keep your healing momentum going using your end of group materials:

- 40-Day Devotional
- "According to the KING" Bookmark
- EWO Final Prayer Document.

Tools to Grow You Spiritually

OTHER GREAT RESOURCES!

If you have been blessed by this program and would like to continue growing spiritually, check out some other great resources we have to offer.

REACHING NEW HEIGHTS: Take your spiritual journey to the next level! Whether you're a seasoned Christian, a new believer, or somewhere in-between, this program is for you.

Reaching New Heights is a 14-week, guided, one-on-one, mentoring experience that's designed to grow you spiritually. Registration includes mentor/disciple pairing and other tools and resources to guide your journey. Time commitment: is approximately 1-hour each week for 14-weeks.

To learn more about this program and to get plugged in, **go to <u>livingintruthministries.com</u> and click on the MENTORNING page.**

LIVING IN TRUTH DAY BY DAY: The Word of God is living and active, our handbook for everyday life. When day to day experiences are viewed against the backdrop of biblical truth, we become aware of the deep spiritual lessons life has to offer. With each revelation, God turns our ordinary into extraordinary!

Each daily reading will inspire you to see God at work in your own life and teach you how to live in God's truth day by day.

(Book is available on Amazon in both Paperback and Kindle)

New Names

Priceless

I am precious and honored in the Lord's sight, and He loves me. ~Isaiah 43:4

God paid a great price to ransom me from an empty way of life. ~1 Peter 1:18

Redeemed

The Lord is my Redeemer. He will teach me what is best and will direct me in the ways that I should go. ~Isaiah 48:17

The Lord has swept away my offenses and sins like the morning mist. He has redeemed me. ~Isaiah 44:22

Set Apart

The LORD my God has chosen me to be his treasured possession. ~Deuteronomy 14:2

I have been set apart for the Lord's faithful service. ~Psalm 4:3

Daughter of the King

The Lord Almighty is my Father. ~ 2 Corinthians 6:18

As a child of God, I am an heir and co-heir with Christ. Although I will sometimes suffer, I will also share in God's glory. ~ Romans 8:16-17

As the King's daughter, I have been made glorious. ~Psalm 45:13

Treasured

I am holy to the LORD my God. He has chosen me as His treasured possession. ~Deuteronomy 7:6

God chose to give me birth and has given me His true Word. Out of all creation, I am his prized possession. ~James 1:18

Worthy

God loves me so much that He died for me. ~Romans 5:8

I am God's handiwork. He has prepared good works in advance for me to do. ~Ephesians 2:10

God paid a great and precious price to save me from my empty way of life. It was a price far more valuable than gold or silver. ~1 Peter 1:18

Capable

God works in me to fulfill His good purpose. ~Philippians 2:13

He who began a good work in me will carry it on to completion until the day of Christ Jesus. ~Philippians 1:6

Transformed

Because I am in Christ, I am a new creation. The old is gone and the new has come. ~2 Corinthians 5:17

When Christ appears, I will be transformed, and I will see him as He is." ~1 John 3:2

As I unveil my face and allow the Lord's glory to shine within me, the Lord will be revealed to others. I am being transformed into God's image with ever-increasing glory, which comes from the Lord, who is the Spirit. ~2 Corinthians 3:18

Beloved

God loves me so much that He gave His one and only Son so that I would not perish but have eternal life. God did not come into the world to condemn me but to save me through His Son. ~John 3:16-17

I am God's beloved child. When He appears, I will be like Him, and I will see Him as He is. ~1 John 3:2

Anointed

The anointing that I have received from God remains in me. Through His anointing, He will teach me about all things and He will remain in me. ~1 John 2:27

God Himself will help me stand firm in Christ. He has anointed me and set His seal of ownership on me. He has put his Spirit in my heart as a deposit and guarantee of what is to come. ~2 Corinthians 1:21-22

Victorious

The LORD God is with me. He will fight for me and give me victory over my enemies. ~Deuteronomy 20:4

Through the victory that is mine, given to me by God, I will have the right to eat from the tree of life, which is in the paradise of God. ~Revelation 2:7

God's peace is available to me, even in times of trouble. I take great hope in knowing that God has overcome the world. ~John 16:33

Chosen

I am God's witness and servant. I have been chosen to know Him, believe in Him, and understand that He alone is God. There is no other God. ~Isaiah 43:10

I have been chosen. I am God's special possession. I will declare the praises of Him who called me out of darkness into His wonderful light. ~1 Peter 2:9

Faithful

Guard my life, LORD. I am your faithful servant and I trust in You. You are my God. ~Psalm 86:2

LORD, I have been crucified with Christ and I no longer live but Christ lives in me. Help me to live by faith, for You have loved me given yourself for me. ~Galatians 2:20

Strong

LORD, You are my strength! You make me as surefooted as a deer. Through your strength, I am able to tread upon the heights. ~Habakkuk 3:19

LORD, You are my strength, my song, and my salvation. I will praise and exalt You forever.   ~Exodus 15:2

Beautiful

LORD, You are enthralled by my beauty. I will honor You, for You are my LORD." ~Psalm 45:10-11

LORD, You make all things beautiful. You have set eternity in my heart; even though I cannot fathom what You have done from beginning to end. ~Ecclesiastes 3:11

LORD, my outward appearance is not what is important. For You, O LORD, look at my heart. ~1 Samuel 16:7

Made in the USA
Las Vegas, NV
12 January 2021